LET'S VISIT SRI LANKA

Let's visit
SRI LANKA

JOHN C. CALDWELL

BURKE

First published in Great Britain April 1967
New edition August 1969
Third revised edition September 1979
Fourth revised edition 1984
© John C. Caldwell 1960
New material in this edition © Burke Publishing Company Limited 1967, 1969, 1979 and 1984.

ACKNOWLEDGEMENTS

The publishers would like to thank the following for permission to reproduce the illustrations in this book.

Art Directors Photo Library; B.O.A.C.; Camera Press Ltd.; Sri Lanka High Commission; Sri Lanka Tea Centre; Sri Lanka Tourist Bureau; Adolf Morath; Paul Popper Ltd.; Hamilton Wright.

The cover photograph was supplied by J. Allan Cash.

The publishers are also indebted to Garry Lyle for assistance in preparing this edition.

CIP data

Caldwell, John, C. (John Cope)
   Let's visit Sri Lanka – 4th ed.
   1.   Sri Lanka – Social life and customs – Juvenile literature
   I.   Title
   915.49'3043   DS489
ISBN 0 222 01017 7

Burke Publishing Company Limited
Pegasus House, 116-120 Golden Lane, London EC1Y 0TL, England.
Burke Publishing (Canada) Limited
Toronto, Ontario, Canada.
Burke Publishing Company Inc.
Bridgeport, Connecticut, U.S.A.
Filmset in 'Monophoto' Baskerville by Green Gates Studios Ltd., Hull, England.
Printed in Singapore by Tien Wah Press (Pte) Ltd.

Contents

Map	6
Let's Visit Sri Lanka	7
Geography and Climate	10
The Legend of Queen Sita	16
The Lion Kings	20
How Buddhism Came to Sri Lanka	26
The Tamils	32
The European Invasions	34
The Government of Sri Lanka	39
Life in Modern Sri Lanka	45
A Visit to the Country	53
The Big Estates	65
Fishermen and Miners	71
Schools and Games	75
Legends and Festivals	79
Pilgrimages	88
Things to Remember	91
Index	93

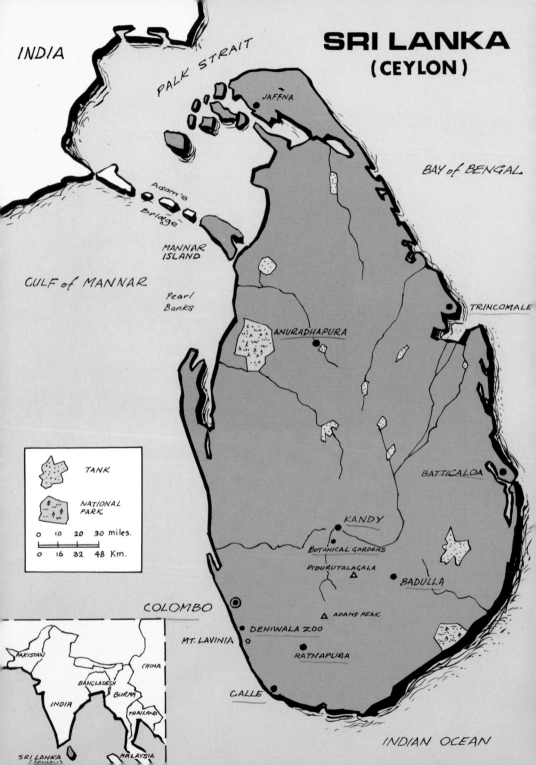

Let's Visit Sri Lanka

Sri Lanka is an island country off the south coast of India. For many centuries it was known as Ceylon but in 1972 its new republican government changed the name to Sri Lanka, which means Resplendent Island. The country has an area of 25,332 square miles (65,610 square kilometres)— that is, almost exactly half the area of England—and a population of over fifteen million.

Although Sri Lanka is small in area and population, it is an interesting and important country. One of the most important of all Buddhist temples is found in Sri Lanka. A tooth of the Lord Buddha who died 2,500 years ago is supposed to be kept in this temple.

And there is a mountain in Sri Lanka named Adam's Peak which is sacred to millions of people. At the top of Adam's Peak there is a place in the rock that looks like a human footprint. Moslems, the people who follow the religion founded by Mohammed, believe the "footprint" was made by Adam when Adam and Eve were cast out of the Garden of Eden.

The mountain is sacred to Hindus, who believe the footprint was made by one of their important gods. Followers of the Buddhist religion declare that Gautama Siddartha, the Lord Buddha himself, made the footprint when he visited Sri Lanka. And finally, many Christians believe that the apostle Saint Thomas visited Adam's Peak.

There are many other interesting things about Sri Lanka. The picture on the opposite page will illustrate one of these. Behind the lorry and to the right is a road sign. This sign is written in the three different languages spoken in Sri Lanka.

Part of the sign is in English. Then the same word is written in a language known as *Sinhala*. At the bottom of the sign the same word is repeated in a language called *Tamil*. The road sign is an illustration of the fact that Sri Lanka is an island of different peoples and languages.

For thousands of years, Sri Lanka has been famous for her precious stones or gems. It is said that the Queen of Sheba and King Solomon sent to Sri Lanka for their jewels. The most important Sri Lankan gems are sapphires, which are usually blue in colour but may also be greenish-blue. One variety, known as the star sapphire, appears to have a bright star inside it. The "star" is really only light reflected from inside the stone.

The largest and most valuable sapphire in the world, weighing 466 carats, was found in Sri Lanka and was bought by a famous American named J. Pierpont Morgan. Another, weighing 400 carats, was bought by a British millionaire. Many other kinds of gems are found in Sri Lanka, too, including rubies and amethysts.

Several thousands of years ago, Sri Lanka was among the richest nations in the world. We will read about those days of long ago and the beautiful cities built by the kings who ruled

**The fact that this road sign is written in three different languages
tells us much more than that the lorry is just leaving a place called
Belihuloya**

them. Now we will learn where Sri Lanka is located and about
its geography and climate.

Geography and Climate

The map shows us that Sri Lanka is an island located in the Indian Ocean. It lies a short distance south of Cape Comorin, the most southerly part of India. Sri Lanka and India are separated by Palk Strait, which is about thirty-three miles (fifty-three kilometres) across at the narrowest point.

There are many rocks and sandbanks between the northern-most tip of Mannar Island and the Indian island of Rameswaram, seventeen miles (twenty-seven kilometres) away. The people have an interesting legend about these rocks and sandbanks which will be described in the next chapter.

Sri Lanka is divided into nine provinces. It is 270 miles (434 kilometres) long and 140 miles (225 kilometres) across at the widest point. The island is shaped roughly like a pear, the northern end being narrower than the southern part. The terrain is flat all along the coast, the land gradually rising towards the middle of the island.

In the centre, but nearer the southern part of the island, is a range of high and beautiful mountains. Adam's Peak, the sacred mountain we have mentioned, is located in this part of Sri Lanka. The highest point on Sri Lanka is Mt. Pidurutalagala, which is 8,281 feet (2,526 metres) above sea level.

In this area, there are four other mountains over seven thousand feet (2,100 metres) high. Fishermen can enjoy very fine rainbow trout fishing in the mountain streams. The rainbow trout is actually a native of the American Rocky Mountains, which means that like all members of the trout family it must have cold clear water in which to live. These fish were brought to the mountains of Sri Lanka about eighty years ago and have done very well.

Sri Lanka is situated just north of the equator. This means that it is a tropical country, and like most tropical countries it has a hot, wet climate. However, because it is a small

Fishing for rainbow trout which thrive in the cold, clear mountain streams

island, there are few parts of Sri Lanka that are very far from the sea: sea breezes help to make the climate less hot.

In southern Asia the word "monsoon" is used to describe the seasons in which rain-bearing winds blow regularly. In Sri Lanka there are two monsoons followed by two inter-monsoon periods. The north-east monsoon is from December to February, when heavy rainfall is limited to the northern and eastern parts of the island. However, thundery showers do occur in the evenings over the western and southern sectors. The south-west monsoon is from May to September when most of the rain is confined to the south-west quarter of the island. In Colombo, the capital city of Sri Lanka, the annual rainfall averages 93 inches (236 millimetres). In one place called Hatton, in the mountains, rainfall averages 140 inches (355 millimetres) a year.

However, there are places in the interior with as little as 55 to 65 inches (140 to 165 millimetres) of rainfall each year.

The lush tropical vegetation which covers these hill-sides is the result of Sri Lanka's hot wet climate

Some of the many varieties of
palm tree which grow in
Sri Lanka

This is called the dry zone. The monsoon winds strike the high
mountains and lose most of their moisture before reaching
these parts of Sri Lanka.

The warm climate and the rainfall make Sri Lanka a very
beautiful island. Sometimes, like Ireland, it is called the
"Emerald Isle", because the country is always so green.

There are many varieties of palm tree on the island of
Sri Lanka, some of which produce food and drink, and other
things used by the people. There are many other tropical
plants, including orchids and tree ferns. These ferns grow so
tall that they actually look like trees.

Sri Lanka is a land of tropical fruits. The climate also makes

13

it possible to grow many crops found only in the warm areas of the world. Tea, cocoa, coconuts, coffee and rice are all important crops.

Although there are over fifteen million people living in a small area, many parts of Sri Lanka are still uninhabited. There are thousands of acres of tropical jungle where monkeys, wild pigs, leopards, black panthers, many species of deer and wild elephants are found.

As we will read later, tame elephants are also common in Sri Lanka. The big animals are captured when young and trained to do heavy work.

Because of its beauty, Sri Lanka is visited by many thousands of European, American and Australian tourists. Visitors from other countries enjoy the tropical beaches and the cool mountains.

Sandy tropical beaches like this one attract to Sri Lanka many thousands of tourists from Europe, America and Australia

Elephants like this one are commonly used for carrying heavy timber which they are taught to carry in their trunks

People also come to see the ancient temples and cities built by powerful kings many centuries ago.

Two dynasties—or lines of kings—ruled, with interruptions by invaders, for over two thousand years. The *Mahavamsa*, or Great Dynasty, lasted from about 483 B.C. to A.D. 304, and the *Chulavamsa*, or Lower Dynasty, ruled from A.D. 304 to A.D. 1815.

15

The Legend of Queen Sita

The earliest written mention of Sri Lanka is in an Indian epic called *Ramayana*. This is a series of stories about an Indian hero named Rama and his many adventures. We might say that the history of Sri Lanka begins with a legend that is found in the *Ramayana*.

According to the legend, Rama's wife was kidnapped by the demon king of Sri Lanka. Rama and his men decided to rescue their Queen Sita. However, Rama did not have enough men to fight the demon king. So he asked Hanuman, the Monkey God, for help, and Hanuman supplied an army of monkeys. Rama and his army of men and monkeys arrived at the strait which separates Sri Lanka from India. They had no boats; but Rama received help from Hanuman.

Hanuman built a series of stepping-stones across the Palk

Straits, so that Rama, his men and his monkeys were able to cross to Sri Lanka and rescue Sita. We have learned that there are many rocks and sandbanks between Sri Lanka and India. According to the *Ramayana*, these are the stepping-stones which were made for Rama and his army. However, other people say that the "stepping-stones" were used as a bridge by Adam and Eve, many centuries before Rama. That is why they are usually known as Adam's Bridge.

Of course we know that both of these stories are legends. All countries have legends with heroes and heroines who did unusual things. Sri Lanka's known history begins about 2,500 years ago when the country was invaded from northern India.

The people who lived in Sri Lanka before the invaders from northern India arrived were called *Veddahs*. Sri Lanka was then a land of wild jungles, and the Veddahs were primitive hunters and fishermen. In 483 B.C. an Indian prince named Vijaya, together with seven hundred followers, landed in Sri Lanka. He married a Veddah princess, named Kuveni, and with her help established himself as a ruler. He had a son and a daughter by her. (There are still a few Veddahs living in the jungles of Sri Lanka. They are very primitive people, wearing little clothing and living almost as they did when Vijaya arrived nearly 2,500 years ago.)

Vijaya eventually deserted Kuveni and her children. He sent an embassy to the Tamil kingdom of Pandya in South India, to fetch the king's daughter to be his queen. The princess came accompanied by seven hundred daughters of the

17

A view across Lake Kandy. Sometimes, Sri Lanka is called the "Emerald Isle", like Ireland, because the country is always so green

principal nobles of the region and they were married to Vijaya and his followers.

Vijaya was the founder of the *Sinhalese* dynasty which ruled Sri Lanka for nearly 2,300 years. This long rule was broken from time to time by periods during which the Tamils assumed power. The first Tamil people came over to Sri Lanka from southern India at the time of the marriage of Vijaya to the Tamil king's daughter. In later history Sri Lanka was frequently overrun by Tamil invaders who on several occasions took over the rule of the country. Today, nearly one-fifth of the Sri Lankan people are Tamils. Of the other four-fifths, the great majority are descendants of Vijaya and his men. They therefore call themselves Sinhalese, and their language is known as *Sinhala*. This name comes from *Sinha*, a word which means lion in the ancient Indian language Sanskrit. The name is found elsewhere in Asia.

The Sinhalese are therefore the *People of the Lion*. As we read about the Lion Kings, we can understand why Sri Lanka is proud of her past.

The Lion Kings

About seven hundred years ago, the famous Venetian explorer Marco Polo visited Sri Lanka. He wrote: "This is better than any other island in the world." As we read about the Lion Kings and their beautiful capital cities, we can understand why Marco Polo was so impressed by Sri Lanka.

For almost 1,200 years the capital of the Sinhalese kingdom was situated in the city of Anuradhapura. This great city covered sixteen square miles (forty-one square kilometres) of palaces, temples and monasteries.

Most of Anuradhapura is still buried in the thick jungle. I once spent two hours driving through the ruins and looking at the buildings made by the Lion Kings. The Brazen Palace, which was built 2,100 years ago, was made with 1,600 stone pillars. There are buildings 300 feet (91 metres) high!

Among the ruins of Anuradhapura, there are several large swimming-pools, bigger than modern Olympic pools. This city is among the largest and best built of all the world's ancient cities.

The Sinhalese kings were not only great city builders; they were good engineers too. In order to provide water at all times of the year and for all parts of the island, they built large reservoirs. These are called *tanks* in Sri Lanka.

Canals were built from the tanks to the fields so that the

This great expanse of water, which actually covers 6,000 acres (2,430 hectares), is one of the *tanks*, or reservoirs, built by the Lion Kings

land could be irrigated. These tanks, many of which are still in use, are remarkable in that they were made without any modern equipment. There were no bulldozers or tractors two thousand years ago. All the work was done by hand. One reason why there are only a few Veddah people in Sri Lanka now is that the Sinhalese kings forced these people into work-gangs. Thousands of Veddahs died during the building of the tanks, and the palaces and temples of the Lion Kings.

Another royal building which can still be visited is the fortress palace of King Kasyapa. This is built on top of a huge rock 1,100 feet (335 metres) high. The story of Kasyapa and the Fortress of Sigiriya is interesting.

Kasyapa was one of the two sons of King Dhatusena who ruled in A.D. 460. Often there was fighting and murder among

Ruins at the summit of Sigiriya where King Kasyapa and his men built their fortress

the members of royal families. Kasyapa arranged to have his father murdered and drove his brother Mogallana into exile.

However, Kasyapa was afraid that his brother would return and avenge their father's death; so he left Anuradhapura and built his palace and fort on the very top of Sigiriya.

For eighteen years Kasyapa and the men loyal to him lived on top of the rock. You can see that it is very steep. I visited the fortress and climbed up to see the ruins of Kasyapa's palace. New steps have been made in the side of the rock, and there is a guard-rail to keep people from falling. Even so, it is a frightening climb.

Kasyapa and his men had no guard-rail. You can still see the tiny steps which they used to climb the rock, which is almost straight up and down.

On one side of Sigiriya are the famous wall paintings of beautiful women. No one knows who made these paintings (which are known as *frescoes*) on the side of the fortress rock. It is thought that perhaps one of King Kasyapa's guards, on look-out duty, painted the lovely women to pass the time away while he was guarding the fortress.

The Sigiriya frescoes were painted between 1,400 and 1,500 years ago and are among the most beautiful works of art in the world.

In time, Kasyapa's brother returned from exile, and the men on the fortress rock had something to do besides paint. There was a great battle, each side using elephants. Kasyapa's men were defeated; and, rather than be captured, Kasyapa committed suicide.

Three hundred years after Kasyapa's death, Sri Lanka was invaded by the Tamils, the people of southern India. The Sinhalese kings fled from Anuradhapura, and built a new capital at Polonnaruwa.

During the eleventh century, the greatest of all the Lion Kings came to power in Polonnaruwa. His name was Parakrama Bahu the Great (his mother was Sunetra Devi, a Tamil from India), and he was a great builder and warrior.

King Parakrama's armies invaded India and defeated the Pandyan kings of southern India. Then Parakrama set sail with a fleet of ships and attacked the kings of Burma. Parakrama also built beautiful palaces and temples and rebuilt many of the tanks which had been damaged. Many of the works of this king can still be seen at Polonnaruwa.

After Parakrama's death, the Sinhalese kings began to lose

It is a frightening climb to the top of the Fortress

These famous Sigiriya frescoes were painted about 1,500 years ago

their power. There were more invasions from India. The capital was moved from place to place.

The Sinhalese Dynasty ended in 1815, exactly 2,319 years after it was founded by Vijaya. Later we will read about the last capital and how the Sinhalese Dynasty ended. First let's learn about the most important event that occurred during the years of Sinhalese rule. This took place in 307 B.C. when a young Indian prince arrived in Sri Lanka. He did not come with an army. Rather, he brought the religion which a majority of people still follow.

25

How Buddhism came to Sri Lanka

Prince Mahinda, son of the Emperor Asoka of India, came to Sri Lanka in 307 B.C. He brought with him the Buddhist religion.

Buddhism was founded by Siddartha Gautama, who was born in Nepal, a little country north of India, about 2,500 years ago. Siddartha Gautama came from a rich family—tradition has it that at the age of sixteen he was given three different palaces.

Although he was rich, the young man was disturbed because so many people were poor and sick. He could not understand why some people were wealthy while so many others did not even have enough to eat.

Gautama decided to find the secret of happiness. He spent time praying and fasting and lived as a hermit in the jungle. Then he sat for forty-nine days under a bo-tree (a kind of fig tree), meditating and without taking any food. While sitting under this tree, he believed he received revelations about how men should live so that there would be no sorrow, no poverty and no unhappiness.

According to the Buddha, sorrow came because there was so much evil in men's minds. If all the evil were uprooted, everyone would be happy and would achieve *nirvana*. This for Buddhists is the perfect existence. We might call it heaven on earth.

The Buddha began to preach and teach, travelling to many

26

places in India. He taught that people should not be greedy, should not lie or even talk lightly, should not kill one another or any living thing. Buddhism is somewhat like Christianity, for in both of them love is important. If people love their neighbours, love animals, stop all killing, they will be happy. The evil and suffering in the world will disappear when hate and greed are gone.

The Buddha attracted many followers. After his death, even more people became Buddhists. When the Emperor Asoka of India became a Buddhist, the religion attracted ever more followers. Asoka sent Buddhist monks to other countries, and soon the religion was among the most important in Asia.

After the Buddha's death, his followers changed many of his teachings to suit their own ideas. There was no written record of what he actually had taught, so it was easy for people to add their own ideas. Buddhists began to build temples. They made large images and worshipped these. Many of the images were supposed to be in the likeness of the Buddha or to show events that had happened during the Buddha's life.

After a while, the Buddhists began to add images of other gods and goddesses so that the temples were filled with idols. The monks in charge of the temples taught people to worship the images and to bring food, money and other tributes for the gods.

Because the Buddha was thought to have received his revelations while sitting under a bo-tree, this tree became sacred to Buddhists. In Sri Lanka, wherever you find a bo-tree, no matter

Behind this wall is the sacred bo-tree of Anuradhapura. It is 2,300 years old

if it is very small, there is usually a temple or shrine built at its base.

The most sacred and important of all bo-trees is in Sri Lanka. The daughter of the Emperor Asoka brought to Anuradhapura a branch of the tree under which the Buddha had fasted and received enlightenment. The tree is still alive. I visited it when I was in Sri Lanka. It is now about 2,300 years old.

We have read that Prince Mahinda, son of the Emperor Asoka, visited Sri Lanka in 307 B.C. He came to a place called Mihintale where the Sinhalese king was enjoying a hunt. Mahinda preached to King Devanampiya Tissa, who was so pleased with the ideas he heard that he became a Buddhist. Soon many of his subjects also became converted.

It was easy to convert the people because at that time the

religion practised in Sri Lanka was Hinduism, and Buddhism was simply a development of this. Furthermore, the Emperor Asoka, who was a powerful ruler of vast regions of India, had recommended this new religion personally to the Sinhalese king, and had sent a royal prince as his missionary. All this had helped to impress King Tissa, and once he became converted the people naturally followed him. Within two hundred years, the Sinhalese had been completely converted. Soon the most beautiful buildings in the ancient cities of Anuradhapura and Polonnaruwa were Buddhist temples, monasteries and *dagobas*.

In the picture on page 90, there is a large building, circular at the base and tapering to a sharp point at the top. In many parts of Asia, buildings like this are used to house relics of Buddha or of some Buddhist holy person. They are called *stupas* or *topes* in most countries, but Sri Lankans call them *dagobas*.

There are dagobas in Anuradhapura and Polonnaruwa and on the top of the mountain at Mihintale where Mahinda first preached about Buddhism.

It is because of Buddhism that Sri Lanka is an important country. Just as Rome is the most important place for Catholics everywhere, so Sri Lanka is the most important country in the Buddhist world. There are different kinds of Buddhists. The Buddhists of Sri Lanka more nearly follow the teachings of Buddha than do those of China, Korea and Japan.

We have learned that during the reign of Emperor Asoka of India, Buddhism spread to many countries. Buddhist monks travelled to China, then to Korea, and finally to Japan. They crossed the Indian Ocean to the islands of Indonesia and the countries of South-east Asia. At one time, much of Asia was Buddhist.

However, in time, people either accepted new religions, or Buddhist beliefs changed. In India, where the Buddha preached and taught, there are now very few Buddhists. In Japan, a country which began to learn about Buddhism in

The richly decorated interior of a Buddhist temple

the eighth century, there are over two hundred different Buddhist sects, most of them with beliefs quite different from those the Buddha taught.

The Sinhalese, however, became Buddhists 2,300 years ago, and most of them have remained true to the religion.

There is one other reason why Sri Lanka is important to the followers of the Buddha. Buddhists are taught that after the Buddha's death parts of his body were taken and placed in certain temples. The most sacred of all these temples is located in the city of Kandy in Sri Lanka. This temple is known as the Temple of the Tooth because Buddhists believe that one of the Lord Buddha's front teeth is in the temple. Later we will learn the interesting legend of the Sacred Tooth and about the festival that takes place once each year when the tooth is taken from the temple and paraded through the streets of Kandy.

We should understand that Buddhism had important effects upon Sri Lanka's history. Because of Buddhism, Sri Lanka remained a nation different from nearby India, where this religion almost disappeared.

The Buddhist teachers brought a new language to Sri Lanka. Buddhist scriptures were written in a language called *Pali*. In order to read the scriptures, many people learned this language. Many Pali words were borrowed and became a part of the Sinhala language.

Now let's read about other people and religions that came to the island.

The Tamils

The Lion Kings made Sri Lanka a prosperous country. With water from the tanks it was possible to irrigate the whole country throughout the year. Then, too, the precious gems found on the island became known to peoples all over Asia and added to the country's wealth.

It is not surprising that outsiders invaded the island. They wanted to conquer Sri Lanka, with her prosperous farms and great cities. Still other people came, not to conquer, but to enjoy the prosperity of the country. If you travel through Sri Lanka, you will see people called Moors, of Indian rather than Arab descent, who came as traders. They are Moslems and their language is Tamil. You will also see Malays whose ancestors came from Java: they are also Moslems but their language is Malay.

Other than the Sinhalese, the largest group in Sri Lanka are the Tamils, who have maintained their separate identity despite their close racial, religious and cultural links with the Sinhalese. They are concentrated in two of the nine provinces of Sri Lanka—the Northern and Eastern provinces.

At one time three powerful Tamil kingdoms, Chera, Chola and Pandya, flourished in South India.

The first important Tamil invasion occurred in about 205 B.C. when Elara, a Chola prince, conquered Anuradhapura and ruled the northern part of Sri Lanka.

After Elara there were four other invasions by Tamils from the Pandya kingdom, and at times Sri Lanka was divided, with parts of it under the rule of the Sinhalese kings, and parts under the rule of the Tamils. The last four kings of Sri Lanka were Tamils and the three immediately preceding them had Tamil mothers.

Because of the many invasions, and because India and Sri Lanka are so near one another, there are now about three million Tamils living in Sri Lanka. Their written and spoken language is different from Sinhala. Remember the picture at the beginning of the book? Now we know the reason for two of the languages on the road sign. There are so many Tamils in Sri Lanka that most signs are written in both Sinhala and Tamil. In the next section we will read why English is the third language of the people.

The Tamils differ from the Sinhalese not only in language but also in religion. They are followers of the Hindu religion of India.

Still another group of people, the Europeans, presently invaded Sri Lanka. Like others who came to the island, they too had an important effect upon Sri Lanka's history.

The European Invasions

The first European to visit Sri Lanka was Marco Polo. He travelled to China in 1271 and stayed at the court of the Chinese Emperor Kublai Khan for seventeen years. When Marco Polo returned to Venice, he travelled by sea. This voyage took three years, and he visited Sri Lanka during the journey.

However, it was another two hundred years before the island became settled by Europeans. Then Sri Lanka was reached by Portuguese seamen who had sailed round the Cape of Good Hope and crossed the Indian Ocean in search of the spices of India and Indonesia. In the year 1505, the Portuguese landed in Sri Lanka. During this period the Sinhalese kings were weak and were fighting among themselves.

A view of Colombo, one of the modern cities built by the European invaders. The clock tower has been used as a lighthouse for a hundred years

They did not have guns or any modern weapons of war. So it was not difficult for the Portuguese to conquer the parts of Sri Lanka near the coast. Although never able to conquer all of Sri Lanka, the Portuguese ruled much of the island for a hundred and fifty years. During this time many people were converted to the Catholic religion.

In 1658 the Dutch, who at that time were a powerful European nation, drove the Portuguese from Sri Lanka. The Dutch did a great deal to improve life in Sri Lanka. They built canals, repaired some of the ancient tanks, and began to cultivate cinnamon, a very important spice. The Dutch also converted to Christianity the people who lived along the coast. There are over one million Christians in Sri Lanka now, the descendants of people who became Christians during periods of Portuguese, Dutch and British rule. About 40,000 of these are of Dutch descent. There were many more of them until fairly recently, when large numbers emigrated to Australia and elsewhere, because of the Sinhala Only Act. (The Act introduced Sinhala instead of English as the official language of Sri Lanka, so that English-speaking Sri Lankans of Dutch descent—known as Burghers—expected to lose their employment and could no longer find schools at which their children would receive instruction in English.)

In 1796 the Dutch lost Sri Lanka to the British, and the country remained under British control until after the Second World War.

However, it was not until 1815 that a treaty was signed

in Tamil between the British and the last Sri Lankan king, whose capital was at Kandy. An interesting story is told about how this king was persuaded to give up his power.

There is a Sinhalese legend which says that the capital city of Kandy could never be conquered unless the invader was able to bore through a rock mountain. The British began to build a road from Colombo to Kandy. They decided at one place to make the road go through part of the mountain. British engineers dug a tunnel through a very large rock ridge, and to this day if you travel by car from Colombo to Kandy you go through this tunnel. When the Sinhalese saw the tunnel, they were willing to let the British have the city of Kandy.

By the end of the nineteenth century, Britain was a great colonial power. Her colonies included all of Pakistan, India, Burma, Sri Lanka and Malaya. (It is interesting to note in passing that the first person in all these countries on whom she conferred a knighthood was a Sri Lanka Tamil.) All of these colonies were given independence after the end of the Second World War. Although in some countries bitterness is felt against the British, in Sri Lanka the people look back without hatred—some actually with nostalgia—to the time of British rule.

The British built many roads and railways, as well as schools, hospitals and churches. They planted the first coffee and rubber plantations. During this period, too, Sri Lanka became one of the world's great producers of tea.

Colombo's artificial harbour. From here, one of Asia's busiest ports, Sri Lanka ships tea, rubber and other exports

In 1931, Sri Lanka became the first country in the whole of Asia to enjoy universal suffrage. This means that all its adult citizens had the right to vote. Today, all those over the age of eighteen are entitled to vote.

In the many schools founded by the British, English was used in teaching. It became the language of education, of government and of business. Sri Lanka in this way came to have its three languages. Sinhala is the language of the majority; Tamil is the language of about four million people, the Tamils and the Moors; English is the language spoken by the Burghers and by almost all educated people, whether they be Sinhalese, Tamil, Moor or Malay. Now we can understand the reason for the English words on the road sign!

38

The Government of Sri Lanka

In all the colonies of Great Britain there were people who wanted freedom and independence. Recently, almost the last British colonies have been given their independence.

When independence is granted, the new nations may remain members of the Commonwealth, if they so desire. Some countries which make this choice are called dominions, because they accept the British sovereign (now Queen Elizabeth II) as their head of state.

However, some of the countries which once were colonies decide not to be dominions. Instead, they prefer to choose their own heads of state, usually by democratic election, and so become republics.

We have read that in 1931 Britain granted the Sri Lankan

people the right to vote. In 1946, they were granted a constitution very like the British constitution; and in 1948, their country became the Dominion of Ceylon, in which the British government was represented by a Governor-General.

However, some of the country's political leaders disliked dominion status. Instead, they wanted a republican form of government; the majority of the people seemed to agree with them. So, in 1972, the Dominion of Ceylon became the Republic of Sri Lanka. This means that the head of state is now a president and that Britain has no part at all in the government, although the republic remains a member of the Commonwealth.

Remembering the history of Sri Lanka, can you guess what animal appears on their flag? The flag of the land of the Lion Kings has a golden lion in the centre, against a dark red background within a golden border. It also has the Buddhist bo-leaf in each corner, and on the edge nearest the flag-pole two stripes of green and orange. The stripes represent the two main racial minorities: the Tamils and the Moors.

The constitution of Sri Lanka is democratic, providing all the freedoms which democracies enjoy. The parliament has 174 members who sit for terms of six years. Most of the members of parliament (168) are elected by all citizens over eighteen years of age. The other six are appointed by the president.

The leader of the majority party in the Parliament is the prime minister. His party has the right to rule the country

The British coat-of-arms above the portico shows that this building goes back to the time when Sri Lanka was the Dominion of Ceylon. The building was then the seat of the Dominion's Parliament

until the next election. However, the prime minister has a less important position than his counterpart in Britain, since the president is allowed to be a very active member of the government and to control it, if he wishes to do so.

Partly because Sri Lanka is small, her government and people have been able to accomplish many things. Sri Lanka's achievements are unusual in Asia where so many people and governments are poor. In Sri Lanka, all education is free, from kindergarten to university. This means that most people can read and write and are better educated than those of neighbouring countries. Sri Lanka is also one of the healthiest countries in Asia where tropical diseases such as cholera and malaria take the lives of many people. Comparatively few Sri Lankans suffer from these diseases.

41

Language is a problem in Sri Lanka. The Sinhalese majority want theirs to be the official language and the only one, other than English, taught in schools. The four million Tamil-speakers are not happy with this idea. They want their children to learn Tamil as well as English. (There was actually a time when the British had considered Tamil the official language.)

In May 1958 there were outbreaks of violence and riots. The language dispute and a demand for local self-government by the Tamils were partly the cause. The riots lasted for two

One of Sri Lanka's six universities. These universities have no fee-paying students, for in Sri Lanka all education is free

days until the Governor-General was forced to declare a state of emergency throughout the island, taking over the administration, and entrusting the maintenance of order to the army.

Such disputes between the Sinhalese and the Tamils have continued under the republican government, and the problem has grown more serious as many of the Tamils now wish to govern themselves in a separate, independent state. In 1977, this led to rioting and a period of serious violence between the Tamils and the Sinhalese. The country became rather more peaceful after these troubles, but ill-feeling continued, and led to another period of violence and rioting in 1983. This caused many deaths and injuries, and much damage to property. The problem of satisfying the Tamils is still unsolved.

However, we should not believe that all Tamils and Sinhalese are unfriendly to each other. In fact, they often intermarry, and I have visited homes shared by Tamil and Sinhalese families who bear no ill-will towards each other.

Unfortunately, politicians add to the problems. Some Sinhalese political leaders demand that all the Tamils be sent to India. This would not only be unfair to people whose ancestors, like theirs, came to Sri Lanka centuries ago, it would also be impossible for they have severed their connection with India and have become permanently settled in Sri Lanka.

Even though Sri Lanka is more fortunate than her neighbours, the standard of living is far below that enjoyed by most western countries. Remember that one section of Sri Lanka receives much less rainfall than the coastal and mountain areas. One problem is to provide water throughout the year for the dry zone so that better crops can be raised, but this is gradually being solved by irrigation schemes. The biggest of these schemes, on the river Mahaweli Ganga, is providing water for nearly one million acres (405,000 hectares) of farmland, and by 1984 will also be supplying several million people with hydro-electricity.

Another problem is that many Sri Lankan farmers are still using primitive methods of farming. They do not have modern knowledge of fertilizers, insect control and crop rotation. Farmers are quickly learning to use modern equipment and recently excellent results have been achieved.

Foreign governments are helping the people to solve some of these problems, many with loans or grants. Other countries have given gifts in kind, such as tractors and diesel engines. Through the economic aid programme, foreign experts go to Sri Lanka to teach new methods. Foreign doctors are showing the Sri Lankans how malaria can be wiped out. Foreign engineers are helping to repair old tanks so that water can be supplied to farmers in the dry zone and also to make the irrigation and hydro-electricity schemes successful.

Foreigners go to Sri Lanka as a part of this aid programme. And many young Sri Lankans train in neighbouring countries, or go to Britain, America or Australia to study at the universities.

Life in Modern Sri Lanka

The capital of Sri Lanka is Colombo. This city owes its importance to its position as a seaport and airport. It has been described as "the Clapham Junction of the East". With its outer suburbs, it has a population of about 1,400,000.

Colombo is a clean city of wide streets. Many of these streets are lined with rain-trees—so called because the leaves curl up at night; when they open in the sunlight, a shower of rain falls, from the dew caught during the night.

The next largest cities after Colombo are Jaffna, in the Tamil Northern Province, and Kandy, the capital of the Central Province, which is famous for the Temple of the Tooth.

The unit of currency in Sri Lanka is called the *rupee*, as in both India and Pakistan. The Sri Lankan rupee is divided into one hundred *cents*.

Although Sri Lanka has many modern conveniences, people

still follow old ways. For instance, the trains of Sri Lanka have modern diesel engines and air-conditioned carriages, yet here and there in this book you can see pictures which show that people still travel by ancient forms of transport.

A busy street in the city centre of Colombo, showing some of Sri Lanka's more modern means of transport

These villagers on the East Coast still rely on the age-old ox-drawn cart for transport

Big double-decker buses are also part of city transportation, and there are many taxis, too. In Sri Lanka, if you ride in a taxi, you pay according to the size of the car. There are many smaller English-built cars as well as the big American models. The bigger the taxi, the higher the fare.

One of our pictures shows the kind of old-fashioned cart

47

An old-fashioned rickshaw. These are still sometimes seen in Sri Lanka. The rickshaw was actually first invented in Japan — by an American who had it built so that his invalid wife could travel in comfort

that is still often used by country people. The carts are used to carry things from farms to market and also for people who wish to travel from one village to another.

Although the ox is the animal used most of all in Sri Lanka, the water buffalo is also an important work animal, used in farming and sometimes to pull carts.

The water buffalo is larger than the ox, has large sweeping horns, and loves water and mud. When the day's work is done, it is the job of boys and girls of farm families to drive the water buffaloes to the nearest tank or river. The big animals love to lie for hours in the muddiest places they can find.

Wild elephants are still often seen in the jungles of Sri Lanka.

Water buffaloes, useful all-purpose farm animals

Some of these have been tamed and are called "working elephants". Often, when you travel in Sri Lanka, you will see working elephants walking along the highway. They wear bells round the neck and make a jingling sound as they walk. Elephants are used for carrying heavy timber and logs, and for pushing down trees when new land is being cleared. They are trained to pick up big logs with their trunks and to put the logs into a truck.

Elephants love water as much as do the water buffaloes. Every day when the work is finished, the boys and men who handle the elephants, and who are called *mahouts*, drive the big animals to the nearest tank or river. In most places, elephant bathing-time begins at three o'clock in the afternoon. The elephants are very unhappy if they miss their bath. They will lie in the water for a long time, squirting themselves and one another and having a very good time. The mahouts like to make a little extra money, so, for one or two rupees, they sometimes offer an elephant ride to passing tourists.

There are some performing elephants in Sri Lanka, too. In Colombo there is a wonderful zoo, with animals and birds of many varieties. Every afternoon, at five o'clock, trained elephants put on a show. This is called "The Elephant Circus", and boys and girls come by the hundreds to watch the elephants do their tricks.

Sri Lanka is a wonderland for naturalists. Almost every variety of tropical plant grows on the island. All the important

50

After a hard day's work, this elephant likes nothing better than to bathe in the river

animals of India, except the tiger and the rhinoceros, are
found there. Some hunting is allowed, but there are several
national parks where no living thing may be killed.

Everywhere one goes, even in big cities, there are birds.
Thousands of small house-crows inhabit the towns. These
crows are not afraid of people and are very noisy; but no one
would think of harming them. This typifies the attitude of the
people towards birds and animals. It stems from the Buddha's
teaching that men should not kill animals. Some Buddhists
will not even kill an ant or a fly.

A Visit to the Country

Nearly eighty per cent of Sri Lanka's population live on farms or in small villages. To learn more about the life of the people, let's pretend to take a trip from Colombo to Kandy and then into the high mountains.

At first the highway crosses stretches of lowland. On each side of the road there are coconut palms. In Sri Lanka this crop covers more land than any other. Later we will learn of the several varieties of coconut palms and of the products that come from this important tree.

Rice is another very important crop. Sri Lankan farmers grow rice wherever land is suitable. Since rice must grow in

These are paddy fields. The water in which the rice grows can be seen quite clearly in the foreground

Transplanting rice seedlings. Paddy farming is wet and muddy work!

water, lowland (which can be easily irrigated) is best. There are over two million acres (810,000 hectares) of land planted with rice. The rice-farmers of Sri Lanka grow over two million tons (2,323,000 tonnes) of rice each year! However, that is still not enough to keep the people fully supplied with their main food. Sri Lanka must still buy some of its rice from other countries.

The correct word for rice when it is growing in the fields is *paddy*. The fields, filled with water, are known as paddy fields. When paddy is harvested and husked, it is correctly called rice.

Paddy farming is wet and muddy work. A variety of rice called "dry paddy" does not require water. However, the rice of Sri Lanka is the kind that must be grown in water. Paddy is first planted in small seed-beds. When the seedlings are six to ten inches (15 to 25 centimetres) high, they are transplanted into the larger fields. These have already been ploughed and cultivated. Many farmers use modern equipment in paddy farming, but the most commonly used ploughs are old-fashioned, pulled by oxen or water buffaloes. Harvesting is sometimes done by hand too.

Wherever they may live, all Sri Lankans who can afford it eat rice. With their rice, people almost always have a curry dish. Many Sri Lankans have curry and rice for breakfast, for lunch and for dinner.

Curry powder is sold in most grocers. If you look at a box of curry powder, you will probably find that it is made from coriander, turmeric, cumin, cinnamon, fenugreek, black pepper, allspice, red pepper (chilli), nutmeg, cloves and cardamom. These are all varieties of spices.

The curry powder used in Sri Lanka is different from that which we buy. Ours is ready-mixed, but a Sri Lankan house-wife mixes her own. Instead of one box of curry powder made from different spices, a housewife in Sri Lanka will have many different spices from which she makes all kinds of curries. She mixes curry powders to go with vegetables, fish or meat.

Sri Lankan curry is very spicy, and it is often made with lots of red pepper. Sometimes foreign visitors find it so hot that they cannot enjoy it. There is a way of knowing whether the curry you are about to eat is too hot. If the curry is light-coloured, either green or yellow, it will be fairly mild to the taste; if the colour is red, it will be hot!

Curry powder is put on top of the fish, meat or vegetables in a pan and blended into a gravy with coconut milk. This is then cooked into a curry and served with boiled rice.

In Sri Lanka almost everyone, rich or poor, eats with his fingers, using only one hand. A foreigner finds this messy, because he does not know the art of mixing the curries with the rice, lifting a portion with his fingers and putting it into his mouth. The people of India, Pakistan, Burma, Indonesia and other countries in South-east Asia also eat with their fingers. In fact, there are many more people in the world who eat with their fingers than those who use knives and forks.

Western foods are eaten in Sri Lanka, but rice and curries are the most important parts of lunch and dinner. Various preparations made from rice-flour are used for breakfast and often for dinner. Sometimes a salad made of fresh vegetables

Sometimes farmwork is still done by the old traditional methods. Here, paddy is being threshed – by foot, rather than by hand!

is eaten with the rice and curries. There is also a popular preparation called *sambal* which contains so much red pepper that most foreigners cannot eat it. As we can see, Sri Lankans like their food very spicy.

Around any farmhouse you will see a small vegetable plot. Among vegetables that are popular in Sri Lanka are string beans and a plant called okra. It is the seed-pods of the okra that are used. In Sri Lanka, okra is called "ladies' fingers".

Our picture shows a little girl standing near some large pear-shaped fruit. The people are fortunate in that many varieties of fruit grow in Sri Lanka. The big fruit in the picture

These are jak fruits. On the left of the picture is part of a banana plant. The bananas grow upwards from their stem, rather than downwards as one might expect

is called "jak". It is eaten raw when ripe, and many tasty preparations are made with the unripe fruit. These are very popular with the Sinhalese and often form the main meal of poor people.

Many different varieties and sub-varieties of mangoes are found in Sri Lanka. The best are grown in the Jaffna district, in north Sri Lanka, which is also noted for tobacco and cigars. Along the roadside, or near farmers' houses, we could see jak, mango, banana or plantain, mangosteen and a small delicious fruit called *rambuttan*.

There is also an unusual fruit called *durian* which one can sometimes smell before getting close enough to see it; for the moment the skin is cut, the fruit gives off a smell like rotten eggs! However, in spite of its smell, the durian is actually quite tasty.

Perhaps during our trip we might stop at a little shop and sample the sweetmeats that the children of Sri Lanka love. *Kavun* is a little cake made of rice-flour and palm molasses. *Vadai* is a small doughnut, made of leavened and spiced rice and green gram flour, fried in coconut oil. Another favourite sweet, called *aluva*, tastes a little like fudge, and is made from palm molasses, mixed with white flour and cashew nuts. Still another tasty sweet dish is called *jaggery*. This is the crystallised juice of the palm flower.

Travelling along the highway you would certainly see coconut palms growing in some form or other. There are some coconut plantations which cover vast areas. There are

This Tamil thinks nothing of shinning up the tallest palm tree to collect coconuts

also farmers who grow just a few palms near their houses. There are different varieties of palms and all sorts of uses are made of them. Coconut oil is used for cooking. The branches, or fronds, are used for roofing. Delicious drinks are produced from the flower juice.

If you looked up, you would probably see men climbing the tall palms or crossing from the top of one tree to another. These men are *toddy tappers*.

The job of the toddy tapper is to get the sweet juice which the flower of the coconut palm produces. When all the flowers in one tree have been tapped, the tapper crosses over to another tree by rope. He walks on a low rope and holds on to another higher rope.

All the most popular Sri Lankan drinks except tea come from palm trees. The juice or toddy which comes from the flowers of the coconut, kitul and palmyra palms is a slightly alcoholic drink. Coconut toddy is distilled into a hard liquor known as *arrack* with a 60 per cent alcohol content.

The water of the big royal or golden coconut is also a popular drink. Sometimes it is mixed with lime juice or milk.

Boys and girls living in the country districts are fortunate in many ways. The weather is pleasant. Right outside one's door there may be delicious fruits. Yet the farmers' houses are small and simple. They are usually made of mud plastered over a framework of bamboo or other wood. The roof may be of straw thatch or dried palm fronds. Few farm homes have running water or electricity. Water is brought from a nearby stream or well. Farm women carry the water in earthenware jugs. Sometimes the big jug is balanced on the head, or perhaps it is carried against the hip.

When it is time to do the family washing or take a bath, the nearest stream or tank is used. Often the farm people wash clothes and bathe at the same time.

Farm families grow most of their own food, but it is necessary to buy some things. Farmers who do not have paddy fields go to market for their rice and for cooking oils. In many communities there are special market days. The oxen are hitched to the family oxcart, and off the family goes to the market.

Country children have lots of work to do, helping their

Young boys working in a copra shed. Copra is the dried kernel of the coconut from which oil is extracted

parents with the house- or farm-work. Our picture shows boys working in a typical copra shed. Coconuts are rich in oil, and this oil is an important product of Sri Lanka. The boys in the picture are helping to cut open the coconuts. The oil is found in the kernel, the white inside part; when dried this is called copra. The copra is pressed to obtain the rich coconut oil.

In some of our pictures, particularly those of people doing farm-work under the hot sun, the men and boys are wearing little clothing. In other pictures, boys and men are dressed in European clothes. School children, too, often dress in the Western manner.

However, many country people, especially women, still

A typical Sri Lankan country home with a straw roof, mud walls and no windows

dress in the traditional way. Women wear a long piece of cloth wrapped around the body and fastened at the waist. This is called a *saree* (sometimes spelt *sari*) and is also the dress of women in India and Pakistan. There are many different ways of wearing a saree. Even in a country as small as Sri Lanka, one sees many different saree styles. Sarees for parties and special occasions are often very beautiful in colour and workmanship.

Many Sinhalese men still wear the old-fashioned *sarong*, a piece of cloth wrapped around the waist and looking somewhat like a dress. A similar garment, called a *verti*, is worn by Tamil men.

But as we have said, more and more people today dress in the European style. This is especially true of men living in towns and cities.

Among country people there are many men and women whose teeth are a peculiar and unattractive red colour. This is caused by the chewing of betel. Many people in Asia have this habit; it is somewhat like smoking cigarettes.

Betel is made by placing a piece of nut from the areca palm on a betel leaf. This is then covered and mixed with a little tobacco and lime. The leaf is folded up, and whenever one wants a chew a piece is broken off. The areca nut contains a red dye which, when chewed, discolours the teeth.

As we continue our visit through the country, the road begins to climb into the hills. The way people live in the highlands is like that in the lowlands; but the landscape is

A pepper vine growing on a kapok tree

different. Instead of paddy fields, we now see pepper and cinnamon, cocoa, coffee and rubber trees.

Our picture shows a man standing beside a tall pepper vine. The pepper plant grows as high as twenty feet (six metres), climbing up the trunks of trees. The tree on which this vine is climbing is called a kapok tree. This is a tall, light-coloured tree with a smooth bark. The kapok we use for filling pillows and mattresses comes from the silky white fibres which surround the seeds. This fibre looks like the white fluff we find in milkweed seed-pods.

The cinnamon tree, which grows in this region, is of value more for the bark than anything else, for it is from this that the spice comes.

Much of the land in the hills and mountains is divided into big plantations or estates, rather than into small farms. We will now read about these estates and especially about some of the more important products grown on them.

64

The Big Estates

The word "estate" is more often used in Sri Lanka than the word "plantation". An estate may cover several hundreds or several thousands of acres. In many estates three or four crops are grown together. You may see hillsides covered with rubber trees. Scattered among the rubber trees are coffee and cocoa trees. Along the edges, there will often be rows of kapok trees, often with pepper vines growing up their trunks.

The rubber, cocoa and coffee estates are found in the low hills. Both rubber and coffee were brought to Sri Lanka from South America. The rubber tree grows at any elevation up to 2,000 feet (610 metres). This important tree came to Sri Lanka

Both these women are rubber tappers. The one on the left is Sinhalese, the one on the right is Tamil

almost by mistake. In 1876 the Indian government obtained seeds and small plants from Brazil. The trees did not grow well in India, and a few plants were sent to Sri Lanka, where they did so well that the making of rubber has now become an important industry.

Rubber comes from the latex, or sap, of the tree. A cut is made in the bark. It is not deep, but it extends about half-way round the trunk. The latex flows from the cut into a bowl tied just below it. The bowl is emptied from time to time by the rubber tappers, who are mostly Tamil women.

After the latex is collected it is treated with an acid. Then it may be dried, smoked or shipped in the liquid form. An

Tamil women picking tea which they put into the baskets on their backs. The flush is picked from the tea bushes about once every ten days

estate with big trees may produce as much as 700 lb. (320 kg.) of latex for each acre (0.405 hectare).

Tea is the most important crop grown on the estates. It is by far the most valuable product of Sri Lanka. Nearly one-eighth of all the tea grown in the world comes from Sri Lanka.

Tea is the most popular drink of the British, Russians, Chinese and Japanese and has been used for 1,500 years. Several legends are told about how man first discovered tea. One legend tells of an Indian holy man who prayed without sleep for years, but at last the man became so tired that he fell asleep. When he awakened he was so ashamed that he cut off his eyelids and prayed for another five years without sleep.

One day the holy man became so tired that he felt certain he was going to fall asleep again. He picked some leaves from a shrub near by, and as he chewed the leaves he began to feel wide awake. The people in nearby villages began to chew the leaves, so that they, too, could stay awake. Soon someone had the idea of pouring hot water on the leaves, so that, instead of being chewed, the magic stuff could be taken as a drink. Thus tea was invented, according to the legend.

The people of Europe did not know about tea until Dutch traders brought some leaves from China in the 1700s. The drink soon became very popular, especially in Britain. Now the average consumption of tea in Britain is 11 lb. (5 kg.) per person per year.

Tea grows best in tropical countries where the rainfall is heavy. The best tea grows in hills or mountains. In Sri Lanka there are a few tea estates in the hills under 2,000 feet (610 metres) high. But the very best tea grows at an elevation of 6,000 feet (1,830 metres). The tea bush is related to the camellia, a plant that is grown for its lovely flowers. Wild tea bushes grow to a height of 30 feet (9 metres). The cultivated tea bushes are kept pruned.

There are different kinds of tea, depending mostly on how the leaves are treated. Green tea comes from China. Oolong tea is a variety produced in the high mountains of Formosa. The tea produced in Sri Lanka's mountains is called black tea.

But whatever the variety, the best tea always comes from the *flush*, the name given to the tender new leaves which grow at the end of each branch. If the larger and older leaves were used, the tea would taste bitter. In Sri Lanka almost all the work of picking tea leaves is done by Tamil women. About once every ten days they go among the neat rows of tea bushes and pick the flush.

The baskets full of leaves are taken to the estate factories, and the leaves are allowed to wither for a day or two. The wilted leaves are then crushed by big rollers and placed on tables where they are left to ferment. During this process the colour turns from green to black. Finally the black, fermented leaves are heated in big ovens. After a second firing in ovens at a temperature of 200 degrees Fahrenheit (93 degrees Centigrade), the leaves are sorted and graded. They are then

The best tea grows in hilly districts; these slopes are covered with tea bushes. The building on the left is a factory

ready to be shipped. It takes about forty-eight hours from the time the flush is picked until the tea is ready to be packed.

Green tea is made by putting the freshly picked leaves into the ovens. This is done before the leaves can ferment and change colour.

The youngest leaves are small and tender and make what is known as pekoe tip tea. The next youngest leaf is used to

Tea being withered in a modern factory. "Withering" is the first of the processes which turn the green leaves into the black tea we buy

make orange pekoe. Then, as the leaves become larger, they are used for pekoe tea and a type called souchong.

The tea estates of Sri Lanka are beautiful. Tea bushes planted in neat rows cover large areas. Often you will see the boys and girls who are not at school helping their mothers to pick the tender leaves. The tea bushes do not begin to produce good flush until they are three years old. It is not until the bushes are five years old that they produce a large crop of young leaves.

Each year nearly 207,000 tons (210,000 tonnes) of tea are grown in the mountain estates of Sri Lanka. India is the only country which exports more tea than Sri Lanka. The people call the tea industry the *Mahabadda*. This means the Great Industry. Tea provides work for thousands of people and brings in much of the money Sri Lanka needs to operate her government.

Fishermen and Miners

If you were a girl living in Sri Lanka, you might become a tea picker or a rubber tapper. These are jobs often done by girls and women. If you were a boy, you might become a toddy tapper or else a mahout, taking care of elephants. There are also other important occupations in Sri Lanka that we should know about.

Fishing is an important industry. Good varieties of fish are

A fish seller with his wares. Fish is more popular than meat in Sri Lanka, especially among the Hindus

more expensive than meat, but more people, especially among the Hindus, eat fish than meat. There are many fishing villages along the coast of Sri Lanka. The fishing boats are simple: most of them do not have motors. The fishermen sail far out to sea in their little sailing-boats or in their *catamarans*, which are rafts of three logs tied side by side.

On school holidays small boys often go out to sea with their fathers for the day's fishing, and older boys frequently learn to become expert fishermen.

Another important industry is mining—not coal, but precious stones!

A greater variety of precious stones is found in Sri Lanka than in any other part of the world. As we have said earlier, Sri Lanka has been known for her precious and semi-precious gems for thousands of years. Her sapphires and rubies are famous. Among semi-precious stones found in Sri Lanka are alexandrites, amethysts, aquamarines, cat's eyes, garnets, moonstones, spinels, topazes, tourmalines and zircons.

Our picture shows two men standing by a river bank with long poles in their hands. From the picture, it would be hard to know what these men are doing. In fact, they are miners. The precious stones of Sri Lanka are found near the town of Ratnapura. *Pura* is an old Sanskrit word meaning city, and this name means "the city of gems".

The gems of Ratnapura are found near the surface of the ground. It is not necessary to dig tunnels or shafts. Mining gems in Sri Lanka is very much like panning gold. The miners

These men are "mining" for precious stones

dig up the muddy gravel from shallow pits and then wash it in a small stream. The gems are heavy and sink to the bottom, and they are then collected.

Men who work rough stones into perfect gems are called lapidaries. Our picture shows a Ratnapura lapidary. On the shelf by his side are some big stones from which he will get several beautiful and precious gems.

The people of Sri Lanka are fine workmen. Girls and women

A skilled craftsman at work.
The lapidary knows how to
turn a rough-looking stone
into a beautiful gem

A mask-maker at work in the open air. The Sri Lankans, who are fine craftsmen, are especially good at wood carving

often weave pretty baskets from rice and other varieties of straw. Or they may work in pottery factories, making the various kinds of earthenware jugs that are used in Sri Lanka.

Other craftsmen make lovely objects of lacquer, brass, copper, silver and even gold. Sri Lankan workmen are especially good at carving. They carve all kinds of objects from ivory and from wood. Some of the most popular articles bought by tourists are carved elephants made from the wood of the ebony tree, and cigarette cases and caskets made of tortoise-shell.

Schools and Games

We have learned that boys and girls in Sri Lanka have free education from kindergarten to university. Even as rich a nation as the United States of America does not provide so much free education. This does not mean that all children in Sri Lanka go to school. Children in the remoter country areas, and children of very poor people, sometimes have no schooling.

Boys and girls study all the usual subjects. They have lessons in geography and history, arithmetic and science. At the moment, Sinhalese children study in Sinhala, and Tamil boys and girls study in their language. All boys and girls begin to study English in the primary school. Boys and girls in their fifth or sixth year at school can already speak English.

We have learnt that the British built many schools in Sri Lanka, and English was used in these schools. English is still an important second language, spoken by almost all educated people.

The Sinhala language has fifty-one letters in its alphabet. The letters look peculiar to us, don't they?

The picture showing Sinhala writing is taken from a history book studied by Sinhalese children. The boys and girls learn from this picture how their writing has changed. At the top of the picture are letters written 1,500 years ago. Gradually the letters became rounder, until the bottom picture shows Sinhala letters as they are written now. The history of the

A country school in Sri Lanka. Sri Lanka is proud that ninety per cent of the people can read and write.

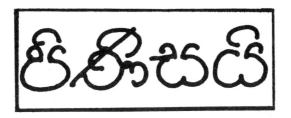

Sinhala language is divided into four periods, and modern Sinhala dates from the middle of the thirteenth century.

Do you remember the picture in the first part of this book which shows Sinhala and Tamil letters on a road sign? To our eyes the letters look similar. Tamil letters have remained unchanged for over two thousand years.

If you lived in Sri Lanka, your last name would probably be very long. Most Sri Lankan surnames have four or five syllables as in Arunachalam or Senanayaka. Many Sri Lankans like to take Biblical and Western-style names. One of Sri

Lanka's Prime Ministers was named Solomon West Ridgeway Dias Bandaranaike.

Boys and girls learn about their unusual history. They are taught how Mahinda brought Buddhism to Sri Lanka in 307 B.C. Several pages of history books tell about the *bhikkhus*, the Sinhalese word for Buddhist priests, and their importance to the country. There are many stories, called *Jatakas*, which tell of happenings in the Lord Buddha's several lives. Buddhist boys and girls learn many Jataka stories. One school exercise is for children to learn at least one Jataka by heart.

Boys and girls in Sri Lanka play the same kinds of games and sports as Western children. The two most popular sports in school are cricket and soccer. Sri Lankan teams have played against national, county and university teams in the U.K., and have done pretty well, too. Rugger and tennis rank next in popularity.

A cricket game in Sri Lanka. It was, of course, the British who introduced the Sri Lankans to cricket

Legends and Festivals

There is a story in the earlier part of this book which tells of how Rama crossed over the sea by way of stepping-stones to rescue Sita. This is one of the many legends which boys and girls learn about in Sri Lanka. A legend is a story that is passed down from generation to generation. Some of these stories are based on fact, while others are not.

The book from which the story of Rama and Sita comes, the Hindu *Ramayana*, is filled with similar stories. Other legends are related to Buddhism, and there are also festivals to celebrate some of the stories.

The biggest festival in Sri Lanka is held in connection with a story about Buddhism. Because of this story, one of the most sacred of Buddhist temples is in Sri Lanka. The story had its beginning in India at the time the Lord Buddha died.

The Hindu people of India believe in cremation. This means that instead of being buried, the dead are burned. Before founding his own religion, the Buddha was a Hindu. When he died, his followers, being Indians who still followed the Indian Hindu custom, burned his body. According to Buddhist legend, several parts of the Buddha's body were not destroyed by the fire. Four teeth, some hairs from his head, and the collar-bones miraculously did not burn.

The unburned parts of the Buddha's body were taken to temples in Burma and India for safekeeping. According to the story, one of the left front teeth became the property of King Guhaseva of Kalinga who ruled a part of North India. The king built a beautiful temple for the tooth, and many people came to worship at the temple.

The Hindu king of Pattaliputra decided to have the sacred tooth destroyed. Messengers were sent to seize the tooth; but when they tried to take it from the temple it shot into the sky, giving out beautiful rays of light and smoke, and frightening all the people who saw this miracle.

However, the messengers eventually managed to get the tooth, and took it to the king. The king tried to burn the tooth but, as soon as he set fire to it, it turned into a lotus flower. He ordered it to be smashed with a big hammer, but the tooth merely sank into the metal. Finally, it shot up into the sky where it began to shine like a bright star. These miracles so frightened and impressed the Hindu king that he became a Buddhist, and returned the tooth to King Guhaseva of Kalinga.

The story of the sacred tooth spread throughout India, and other kings decided they wanted it. So many wars were fought for the tooth that King Guhaseva decided to send it away secretly to Sri Lanka. The tooth was hidden in the hair of the king's daughter, who travelled to Sri Lanka in disguise.

Because of these happenings, the tooth became sacred to all Buddhists. It was kept in a beautiful temple; and whenever the Sinhalese capital was moved, the tooth was also moved. Many stories were told of miracles performed by the tooth. Once when it did not rain for months, the tooth was taken out in a big procession. At once the rain began to fall!

More wars were fought over the sacred tooth. In the thirteenth century it was captured by South Indian invaders and taken back to India. After many adventures, the sacred tooth was brought to Kandy and placed in a special temple— or at least this is what the people of Sri Lanka believe to this day.

It is said that the tooth was really destroyed by the Catholic Archbishop of the Portuguese colony of Goa, on the west coast of India. The Archbishop had the tooth ground into tiny pieces and thrown into the ocean. The Sri Lankans believe that the tooth reassembled itself and returned to Sri Lanka.

Splendidly costumed, the Kandyan dancers carry out traditional movements to the beat of the drum

As a matter of fact, Buddhists everywhere believe that the tooth is still in the Dalada Maligawa, or Temple of the Tooth, in Kandy. Every year during the month of August one of the greatest Buddhist festivals is held in Kandy. It is called the Esala Perahera. Boys and girls enjoy this festival because of all the parades and processions and eating and drinking that goes on. Oddly enough, until the eighteenth century the Perahera was held exclusively in honour of four Hindu deities and had no connection with Buddhism. It was only in 1775 that the festival was given a Buddhist character and incorporated into Buddhist worship.

The tooth is supposed to be kept in a golden casket. The casket is set on a golden throne behind gilded iron bars. I have visited the temple and seen the casket. People may do this each evening. But during the two weeks of the Perahera, the casket is taken out and paraded through the streets of Kandy.

Many Buddhists come from other countries to watch the beautiful processions of the Perahera. A great number of decorated elephants take part in the procession, and the casket is carried on top of one of the elephants called the Maligawa Tusker. There are also bands of musicians, drummers, flame-throwers and dancers.

The Esala Perahera ends on the banks of the Mahawali river near Kandy. This final part is called the Water-cutting Ceremony. The waters of the river are "cut" by priests with

The famous Dalada Maligawa, or Temple of the Tooth, in Kandy

The Maligawa Tusker bearing the golden casket beneath a tall canopy

swords. Then four clay pots are filled with the water, taken to the temple and kept until the next celebration of Perahera.

The Perahera is one of the most beautiful festivals in the world.

There are other important Buddhist festivals. Wesak Night comes during the full moon in May and celebrates the birth and the death of the Buddha. Wesak can be compared to Christmas and Easter in Christian lands. Every Buddhist home is decorated with lanterns, and thousands of people go to the temples to worship.

Over two-thirds of the people of Sri Lanka are Buddhists.

And, as we have said, they are loyal Buddhists. Boys and girls of Buddhist families take part in the festivals and visit the temples with their parents. They light sticks of sweet-smelling incense before the big images of the Buddha and often bring offerings of flowers.

Buddhists do not visit their temples on one day each week, as Christians do who go to church. Instead, temples are visited on special poya days, the Buddhist public holidays. Like Sunday, poya days usually come round four times a month but they are not always seven days apart.

A Perahera official, dressed in richly jewelled traditional costume

These drummers and the gaily costumed elephant form part of the colour and spectacle of the Perahera festival

The Buddhists have many beliefs that seem strange to us. If you were a Buddhist boy or girl, you would take unusual medicines when you became ill. The Buddhist priests, or *bhikkhus*, believe in the effectiveness of ancient, traditional medicines. They use many varieties of herbs when people are ill.

The Buddhists also believe in astrology. This means the monks study the stars in the belief that they influence human affairs. In practical terms, this may mean that a person will visit a Buddhist monk for advice on what day may be best to begin a new business or a long trip. Often Sinhalese families will visit an astrologer to get help.

However, Sri Lanka also has several thousand doctors trained in the latest Western methods, about six hundred well-equipped hospitals and over three hundred dispensaries supplying modern medicines.

We must remember too, of course, that there are many Hindus among the Tamil people. And there are also many Christians and Moslems.

Each of these religious groups has its own special days and festivals. Christians, of course, celebrate Christmas and Easter. Hindus celebrate *Thai Pongal*, a day of thanksgiving, in January and *Deepavali*, the Festival of Lights, in November. Moslems celebrate the Prophet Mohammed's birthday in January and observe *Ramadan*, a month of fasting from sunrise to sunset each day, during the early part of the year.

There is one festival that Sinhalese and Tamils have together. The Sinhalese and Tamil New Years both come in early April. This is a day of celebration and happiness, with visits to neighbours and relatives.

The astrologers are visited, too, on New Year's Day. People believe that at a certain time during the day the body should be rubbed with oil to bring luck. There is also a belief that there is a lucky colour for New Year's Day, and that clothes of this colour should be worn. The astrologer is visited so that he can study the stars and decide on the colour and the best time for putting on the oil.

Pilgrimages

Sri Lankan people like to make pilgrimages to visit one of the old cities or some famous temple. Because Sri Lanka is a small country with a good road system it is possible to reach any part of the island within a few hours. Often the whole family will go on a pilgrimage. While these trips may be made so that the family can worship at a holy place, they are also intended to be enjoyed. A pilgrimage in Sri Lanka is like a big picnic.

The most important pilgrimage is to the top of Adam's Peak, the holy mountain of Sri Lanka. We have read that this mountain is sacred to Buddhists, Christians, Hindus and Moslems.

The climb to the top of this peak, which is more than 7,000 feet (2,135 metres) high, usually begins after supper. It is a long climb, and the object is to reach the top just before sunrise. On the way to the top, the pilgrims sing and chant prayers. A small Buddhist temple stands near the summit, and each pilgrim who reaches the top has the right to ring the temple bell once. If you were a boy or girl living in Sri Lanka, you would be proud of having rung this bell. People who have made the climb several times like to tell of the number of times they have rung the bell.

On one side of Adam's Peak there are some huge chains attached to the rock. The people of Sri Lanka say that Alexander the Great fastened them there when he visited Adam's Peak. Marco Polo climbed Adam's Peak in the thirteenth century and later wrote about the wonderful view that could be had from the summit.

Many other places are visited by families on pilgrimages. When I climbed to the top of the Fortress Rock at Sigiriya, several families were also making a pilgrimage to this famous place. At the end of the pilgrimage, everyone sat down to a picnic lunch.

Each year there is a pilgrimage to Kataragama, which is located in a beautiful jungle spot. People come to this place to pray or sometimes to punish themselves for wrongs they believe they have done. Some people actually torture themselves. Hindus will be seen walking on flaming coals or rolling in hot ashes. While this is going on, drums are beaten, and strange-sounding music is played.

Once a year thousands of people make a pilgrimage to

Anuradhapura for the Poson festival. This is held to commemorate the introduction of Buddhism into Sri Lanka by Prince Mahinda. The pilgrims visit all the most important shrines and everyone has a look at the famous bo-tree.

During Poson, Anuradhapura is once again a city of people instead of ruins. Families camp on the edge of the jungles or among the ruined palaces and temples.

Often several families will plan a pilgrimage together. Or perhaps all the boys and girls in a school will go off together by bus.

The people of Sri Lanka, whatever may be their religion, are proud of their temples, ruined cities and places of beauty.

Kelaniya Temple, just outside Colombo. The white building on the left is a *dagoba*

Things to Remember

Sri Lanka is one of the smallest countries in Asia. It is small in area and in population. We have learned that Christians, Hindus and Moslems live there, but over two-thirds of the people are Buddhists.

The Buddhists of Sri Lanka have followed their religion for more than 2,000 years. Buddhism is important in the daily lives of people, even in the government. Because of Buddhism, Sri Lanka has her beautiful temples and ruined cities. It is Buddhism that has made Sri Lanka and her people different from India and her people.

We have learned some unusual things about Sri Lanka. It is a modern country with fine roads. Her people have the right to free education, and they were among the first in Asia to enjoy the right to vote. Yet because of the religion of the majority, it is a land where people make important decisions by studying the stars and where many people use herbs rather than modern medicines.

Even though the Sri Lankans are more fortunate than many other peoples in Asia, there are still problems to be faced. We

91

Village schoolgirls marching to an athletic event

have read how foreign countries are helping to solve these problems.

We also know that there have been times of trouble between the Tamils and the Buddhist Sinhalese.

Yet, for the most part, our friends in Sri Lanka have enjoyed peace for many years. It is a country to which many thousands of people come from all parts of the world to enjoy the lovely countryside and to see the ancient cities and beautiful temples.

Index

Adam's Peak 7, 10, 88–9
Alexander the Great 89
aluva 58
amethysts 8
Anuradhapura 20, 21, 23, 24, 28, 29, 33, 90
area of Sri Lanka 7
arrack 60
Aryans 19
Asia 19, 29–31, 32, 38, 41, 56
Asoka Emperor of India 26, 27, 28, 29
astrology 86, 87

bananas 58
beans 57
betel 63
bhikkhus 78, 86
birds 52
bo-trees 26, 27–8, 90
Brazen Palace 21
British rule 36, 37–8
Buddha, Buddhism 7, 26–31, 42, 52, 79–87, 88–9, 90, 91–2
Burghers 36, 38
Burma 25, 29, 37, 40, 56

canals 21, 36
Cape Comorin 10
Cape of Good Hope 34
Catholics, Catholicism 36, 81
Central Province 45
Chera 33
China 29–30, 34
Christians 7, 36, 37, 88, 91
Chola 33
Chulavamsa 15
churches 37
cinnamon 36, 55, 64

climate 11, 12, 13, 44
clothes 17, 62–3
cocoa 14, 64, 65
cocnut milk, oil, palms 53, 56, 58–60
coffee 14, 37, 64, 65
Colombo 12, 37, 45, 46, 53
Commonwealth 39
constitution 40
copra 62
crafts 74
currency 45
curry 55–7

dagobas 29
Deepavali 87
deer 14
Dehiwala 45
Devanampiya Tissa, King 28
Dhatusena, King 22
diseases 41–2, 44
dominion status 39, 40
Dravidians 19
drink 60
durian 58
Dutch settlers 36, 67

economic aid 44
education 41, 44, 75–8, 91
Elara, Prince 33
elephants 14, 23, 50, 83
English language 38, 43, 75
Esala Perahera 82–4
estates 64–70

farming 44, 53–5, 58, 60
festivals 79–87, 90

fish fishing 11, 55, 71–2
flag 40
food 55–8, 61
frescoes 23, 25
fruit 13, 58, 60

games 78
Gautama, Siddartha, *see* Buddha
gems 8, 32, 72–3
government 39–44, 91
Governor-General 40, 43
Great Britain 40
Great Dynasty 15
Guhaseva, King 80–81

Hanuman 16–17
Hindus, Hinduism 7, 29, 33, 79–82, 87,
    88, 91–2
hospitals 37
houses 60

independence 39
India, Indians, 10, 16–17, 19, 24, 25, 27,
    30, 32, 33, 37, 39, 44, 56, 63
Indian Ocean 10, 30, 34
Indonesia 30, 34, 56

jak fruit 58
Jaffna 45, 58
jaggery 58
Japan 29
Jatakas 78
Java 32
jewels 8
jungles 14, 17, 20, 48

Kalinga 80
Kandy 31, 37, 45, 47, 53, 81, 82, 83
kapok 64, 65

Kasyapa, King 22–4
Kataragama 89
kavun 58
kitul palms 60
Korea 30
Kublai Khan 34
Kuveni 17

language 8, 31, 32, 33, 38, 43, 75 –7
latex 66–7
leopards 14
Lion Kings 19–25, 32, 40
Lower Dynasty 15

Mahavamsa 15
Mahawali River 83
Mahinda, Prince 25, 28, 29, 78, 90
mahouts 50
Malay language 32
Malaya 37
Malays 32, 38
mangoes 58
mangosteen 58
Mannar Island 10
Marco Polo 20, 34, 89
meat 55
Mihintale 28, 29
mining 72–3
Mogallana 23
Mohammed 7, 87
Monkey God 16
monkeys 14
monks, monasteries 20, 27, 29–30
monsoons 12–13
Moors 32, 38
Moslems 7, 32, 87, 88
Mt. Lavinia 45
Mt. Pidurutalagala 10
mountains 10, 11, 14, 37, 53, 68

names 77
national parks 52

Nepal 26
New Year 87
nirvana 26
Northern Province 45

okra 57
orchids 13
oxen 55, 61

paddy 54
pagodas 29
Pakistan 37, 39, 56, 63
palaces 20, 24
Pali 31
Palk Straits 10, 17
palm oil 62
palm trees 13
palmyra palms 60
Pandya 17, 33
Pandyan kings 24
panthers 14
Parakrama Bahu the Great 24
parliament 40, 41
Pattaliputra 80
pepper, pepper vines 55, 64
Perahera 82–3
pigs (wild) 14
plantain 58
Polo, Marco 20, 34, 89
Polonnaruwa 24, 29
population 7, 8, 14, 19, 33, 45, 53, 91
Portuguese settlers 34–6
Poson 90
poya days 42, 85
precious stones 8, 72–3
prime minister 41

railways 37

rainfall 11–13, 44
rain-trees 45
Rama 16–17
Ramadan 87
Ramayana 16, 79
rambuttan 58
Ratnapura 72
red peppers 55, 57
religion 79–90, 91–2
reservoirs, *see* tanks
rice 14, 53–5, 56, 57, 61
riots 43
roads 37
rubber 37, 64, 65–6
rubies 8, 72
rupees 45

Saint Thomas 7
sambal 57
Sanskrit 19
sapphires 8, 72
saree 63
sarong 63
schools 37, 38, 75–8
Second World War 36, 37
semi-precious stones 72
Sheba, Queen of 8
Sigiriya, Fortress of 22–3, 89
Sinhala 8, 19, 31, 33, 38, 43, 75–7
Sinhala Only Act 36, 42
Sinhalese Dynasty 19, 20, 22, 24, 25, 29,
    33, 34, 37
Sinhalese people 19, 21, 29, 32, 43, 44.
    58, 63, 81, 87, 92
Sita, Queen 16–17
Solomon, King 8
spices 36, 55
stupas 29
sweetmeats 58

Tamil language 8, 32, 33, 38, 42, 43, 44, 75–7
Tamils 17, 19, 24, 32–8, 43, 63, 87, 92
tanks 21–2, 24, 32, 36, 44, 50, 54
tea 14, 37, 67–70
Temple of the Tooth 31, 45, 82
temples 15, 20, 24, 27–8, 29, 80, 84–5, 88–9, 91
Thai Pongal 87
Tissa, King *see* Devanampiya Tissa
tobacco 58
toddy 60
transport 46–8

tree ferns 13
trout 11

vadai 58
vegetables 56
Veddahs 17, 22
verti 63
Vijaya 17–19, 25

water buffaloes 48–50, 55
wild elephants 50
wild pigs 14
working elephants 50